GARNISHING
THE BASICS AND BEYOND

CONSTANCE QUAN

Designed and Illustrated by
S. NEIL FUJITA

An Irena Chalmers Book

CONTEMPORARY
BOOKS, INC.
CHICAGO

To Stan, Elizabeth and Michael

Published by Contemporary Books, Inc.
180 North Michigan Avenue, Chicago, Illinois 60601

Published simultaneously in Canada by Beaverbooks, Ltd.
195 Allstate Parkway, Valleywood Business Park
Markham, Ontario L3R 4T8 Canada

Published by arrangement with

IRENA CHALMERS COOKBOOKS, INC.
23 East 92nd Street
New York, NY 10128

© 1984 by Constance Quan. All rights reserved.
Printed in Singapore by Tien Wah Press (Pte.) Ltd.

LIBRARY OF CONGRESS
CATALOG CARD NO.: 84-070566
Quan, Constance
Garnishing: The Basics and Beyond.

New York, NY: Chalmers, Irena Cookbooks, Inc.
80 p.
F G H I J   8 7 6 5

CONTENTS

VERSATILE TECHNIQUES 23

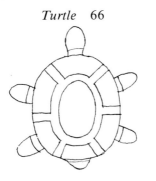

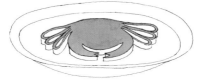

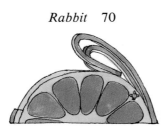

Constance Quan's activities in the culinary arts have involved both home cooks and professional chefs.

As a cooking teacher she has given lectures, demonstrations and classes to enthusiastic amateurs and experienced chefs.

As a food and restaurant journalist she has written more than 200 articles for general public and restaurant industry publications.

She has won distinguished national and international awards for her outstanding food preparations and presentations. They include the Silver Medal of the 1980 International Culinary Olympics held in Frankfurt, Germany, every four years, the Silver Medal of the American Culinary Federation, and the Grand Prize and Judges Award of the Chefs' Association of Westchester and Lower Connecticut. The Société Culinaire Philanthropique, the oldest culinary society in the United States, has honored her with First Prizes in Cuisine, Classical Cuisine, Classical Pastry, Decorative Work and International Dishes.

INTRODUCTION

With surprisingly little time, effort and cost, you can make meals more fun to prepare, serve and eat, using simple, attractive garnishes. Garnishes, the embellishments and decorative touches added to well-prepared food, have long been used by professional cooks to add a finish to plates and contribute subtly to the atmosphere or personality of their restaurants. Simple restaurants have a quick and easy way with a lemon slice, more elaborate ones have staff who specialize in intricate garnishes.

Fine cooking, be it humble or fancy, deserves lovely finishing touches. Good taste and beautiful presentations should go hand in hand. This book is a collection of professional garnish techniques written for both accomplished cooks and novices in the kitchen.

Whether you lean toward good old-fashioned favorites or dazzling newfangled concoctions, whether your specialty is haute cuisine or country style, French, Chinese, Italian, or American cooking at its finest, garnishing will add a new dimension to your culinary style. Breakfasts for the family, backyard barbecues for a crowd, or candlelight dinners for two, can ascend from the ordinary to the extraordinary.

The chapter of this book called *Instant Appeal* shows you how to dress up food when you have barely a moment to spare. You'll be pleased with how much difference even a "jiffy" garnish such as butterflies, miniskewers and twisted citrus slices can make.

In the chapter on *Versatile Techniques,* directions guide you, step by step, in exactly how to make slightly more advanced garnishes. Included are a variety of baskets, deep containers including hollowed pineapple and shallow containers made from cross sections of cucumbers, intriguing carrot knots, graceful cucumber fans, delicately notched wisps of spinach stems, and classic fluted mushroom caps. Through the examples of specific garnishes, you will learn versatile techniques you can use to make suggested variations. In some instances, you may vary the materials, substituting zucchini for cucumber or oranges for lemons. In other instances, you may vary the procedure to create a different look.

Flowers made of fruits and vegetables create an effect both appetizing and gracious. The *Techniques for Making Flowers* chapter shows you how to make lovely single blossoms for trays or platters, as well as colorful bouquets for buffet centerpieces.

Showing Off, the last chapter in the book, focuses on garnishes that are for sheer amusement. When you turn a cucumber into a friendly crab or a watermelon into a proud spread eagle, surely you fool not a single guest, but most definitely you delight each one!

Garnishes heighten expectations, stimulate the appetite and bring much added pleasure to a meal. Now is the time to go beyond cooking delicious food. Sense the wonderful excitement and satisfaction of garnishing . . . add that special finishing touch.

TOOLS FOR GARNISHING

Garnishing is more a matter of an attitude toward food presentation and of techniques than of having specific and unusual tools. The garnishes in this book are made, not with exotic or contrived gadgets, but with a few well-chosen, versatile, fundamental kitchen tools.

While you can make most of these garnishes with just a kitchen knife and cutting board, you may want gradually to acquire the following tools which will make garnishing particularly easy, fun and rewarding. They each will earn their keep in your efficient, well-equipped kitchen because of their multiple uses in both cooking and garnishing.

You will need knives. But don't think a knife is merely a knife! Sizes, shapes and even thicknesses of blades vary.

Fish fillet knife: This knife is designed for filleting flat fish such as flounder or sole; the blade is thin and flexible. The knife is most useful for cutting delicate garnishes because its thin blade allows you to make fine cuts and slices.

Paring knife: A paring knife with a 3-inch blade serves as a versatile all-purpose knife. A handle that has a large grip is easiest to hold and least tiring to use.

Boning knife: A boning knife is usually used for boning meats and poultry. The blade is strong and narrow to allow cutting along the twists and curves of the bone structures. The narrow blade is useful in garnishing when you want to make a narrow cut, such as in hollowing out a deep container. A ham slicer has a narrow blade, too, and is a suitable substitute.

Cleaver: You won't need a heavy chopping cleaver for fine garnishes, but a light, thin slicing cleaver is useful because it has a definite, straight, flat edge that will make carve-and-slice types of garnishes easy to carve uniformly. Any knife with a medium-length straight cutting edge rather than curved blade may be substituted for the slicing cleaver.

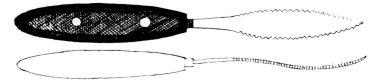

Grapefruit knife: This has a gently bent and serrated blade that is intended for scooping out sections of pulp from a half grapefruit. The bend in the blade helps you cut curved contours and otherwise hard-to-reach places.

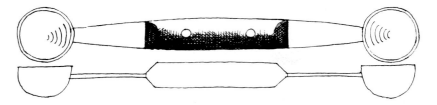

Melon baller: These are available in a range of sizes, from tiny pea-size to walnut-size, plain, fluted, and even oval. The most versatile melon baller is plain, round and about 1 inch in diameter. The key to using it to make full, round balls is to start by cutting deeply into the fruit, rotate the tool, and then come all the way around again to cut a complete ball.

Trussing needle: This tool, designed for tying the legs and wings of poultry to the body for even cooking, is excellent for marking outlines on the skin of watermelons, honeydews or cucumbers for subsequent carving. The needle's flat pointed tip cuts the skin easily, and its long round shape is as easy to hold as a pencil. A metal or wooden skewer may be used instead; even a felt-tipped marker may be substituted.

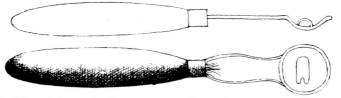

Lemon stripper: Here's a wonderful tool for stripping a twist of lemon peel for sauces or beverages. It is also useful for cutting designs into fruits and vegetables. Sometimes it is called a channel knife, because of the channel it cuts as it removes the skin.

Vegetable peeler: There are as many types of vegetable peelers as there are types of corkscrews. Most work quite well, although each person seems to develop his or her own preference. A swivel blade is easy for most people to use, and suits both left- and right-handed garnishers.

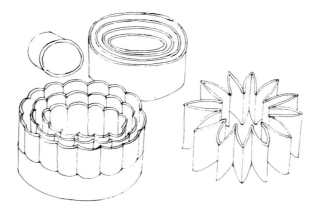

Cutters: A set of concentric circle cutters, ranging from 1 to 4 inches in diameter, can be quite useful. There are plain round cutters and others with fluted edges. Some sets are costly, but round cookie cutters and biscuit cutters can be bought individually and inexpensively. Other shapes useful in garnishing, such as petaled flowers, are also sold individually as cookie cutters.

Skewers, cocktail picks and toothpicks: Wooden skewers, the same ones used for shish kebab, are used in creating centerpieces such as vases of flowers and serving pieces such as the peacock on page 78. A 10-inch length is versatile and can be neatly clipped to shorter lengths with wire cutters, when necessary.

Cocktail picks are short decorative sticks of wood or plastic, used by guests to eat bitefuls of hors d'oeuvres at a stand-up party. They are useful as miniskewers to hold together pieces of fruits and vegetables as garnishes.

Toothpicks can be used in display garnishes such as centerpieces to secure the parts in place. They should be concealed and any excess length trimmed off.

CHOOSING WHICH GARNISH TO USE

As you learn to make garnishes, your repertoire will become quite large. It may take some restraint not to use them all at once!

Be careful not to overdo it by garnishing a dish to the point where the main ingredient is overwhelmed rather than enhanced. Select the most appropriate way to highlight the food you cook, and use the right garnish in the right place.

In choosing which garnish to use, consider the following:

Taste, color, shape: Use garnishes of taste, color and shape that complement the main ingredient of the dish. For example, gherkins taste good with pate, but not very good with fruit salad; orange carrots look attractive with chops, but not as attractive with spaghetti in tomato sauce; round peas and onions give interest to a platter of fish, but look monotonous with a platter of meatballs.

Temperature: Both hot and cold garnishes are compatible with hot foods, but generally only cold garnishes go well with cold foods.

Size: Individual garnishes should be scaled to fit an appropriate single portion. Any garnish arrangement used for a centerpiece should be massive enough to be a focal point of the dinner table or the buffet table.

Mood: Choose and use garnishes according to the mood you want to establish, be it dainty, bold, whimsical, elegant or casual. Most garnishes give different effects depending on how they are used. One carrot knot in a bowl of clear broth can look exotic as a first course for dinner, a few carrot knots in a cold salad can look just right for an informal luncheon, and a heap of them on a crudite plate look casual—perfect for snacking.

Cost: When the budget is tight, use generous bundles of economical carrots or zucchini instead of meager portions of costly asparagus. Choose a material you can use freely.

Time: When you are short of time, it is better to use lemons neatly sliced than mushrooms fluted in too much of a hurry. Choose something that you have enough time to make well.

Skill: Some garnishes will be easier for you to make than others. Enjoy using them often. In the meantime practice, gaining ease and proficiency in the ones you find more challenging.

Function, Function, Function: A garnish should make food more appetizing in appearance, texture and flavor. Its whole function is to heighten the enjoyment of the food. Measure the appropriateness of a garnish by how well it serves that purpose.

Ingredients: To create the most exquisite and satisfying garnishes, select fruits and vegetables not only according to taste, but also according to the visual elements of size, proportion, symmetry, color and texture, both inside and outside.

Temperature: Hard vegetables such as carrots and radishes are easier to work with if they are at room temperature instead of refrigerator-cold. To warm them in a hurry, place them in a pan of warm water for a few minutes.

Trimming a base: To allow a round-bottomed fruit or vegetable to sit straight and stable, trim a thin slice from the bottom. Check to see if the fruit or vegetable is exactly upright. If it is not, trim it again.

Ice water: Soaking garnishes made from such vegetables as leeks, scallions and carrots in a bowl of cold water with a few ice cubes in it will help them to "curl" and "set," as well as keep them crisp until you are ready to use them. These garnishes may be made a day ahead and kept in water in the refrigerator.

Lemon juice: Fruits such as apples and pears turn brown when they are cut and exposed to air. To help keep them white, rub the cut surfaces with lemon juice or dip them into a small bowl of acidulated water—water to which you have added the juice of one lemon.

Blanching: Blanching such vegetables as carrots, broccoli, green beans and leek greens makes them slightly more tender to eat and dramatically heightens their natural color. To blanch vegetables, boil enough water to cover them completely; add the vegetables to the pan; let them boil for 5 to 15 seconds; drain; rinse immediately in cold water to prevent further cooking and to set color; drain; dry.

Throughout this book, directions are given for right-handed readers; if you are left-handed, simply reverse the instructions for each hand.

A NOTE TO FOOD PROFESSIONALS

Garnishing is an effective, economical and easy way to enhance food presentations of every type, and is equally applicable in diners and coffee shops, cafeterias and schools, white-tablecloth restaurants and takeout food businesses. The reasons?

Garnishes please customers.
Attractive presentation of food always adds to the enjoyment of a meal. Garnishes are an essential follow-through to the detailed attention you expect to give to aspects such as decor, lighting, music, service and the development of menus and recipes.

Garnishes set style.
A specific garnish that fits your menu specialty will set a style and could even become the "signature" of your establishment, clearly distinguishing it from all others.

Garnishes give a healthful image.
All the garnishes in this book are created from fruits and vegetables; they add a fresh, healthful, nutritious touch that makes your food even more appealing.

Garnishes cost little.
The materials for making most of these garnishes are very inexpensive. A few cucumbers, carrots, tomatoes or apples go a long way. No special tools or equipment are necessary and the majority of the garnishes are not labor-intensive. They can be learned and produced quickly without the bother and expense of extensive staff training.

Garnishes hold well.
You can prepare most of the garnishes in this book ahead, and then refrigerate or hold them in cold water, ready to be added to dishes at the time of service.

Some garnishes are so simple to make that they can be ready in moments, from ingredients you can keep on hand. They make dramatic differences in the food you serve, giving it . . . instant appeal!

Everyday foods can look lovely with fast and fancy touches. Keep in mind the variety of things available in your cupboard and on your refrigerator shelf. You can dress up the humblest meat loaf or ham sandwich and be able to create wonders when guests come to dinner, even on short notice. There are so many ways other than that overused sprig of parsley! Try some of these:

TWISTED CITRUS SLICES

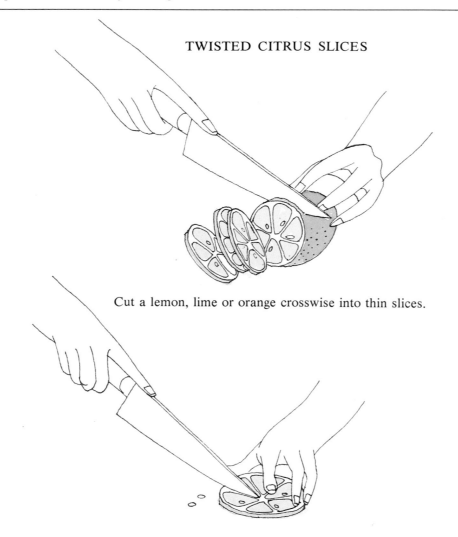

Cut a lemon, lime or orange crosswise into thin slices.

In each slice, make a cut from the center out to the edge.

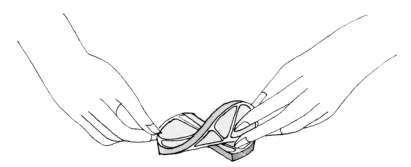

Twist 1/2 of the slice forward and 1/2 of the slice backward.

Place a twisted lemon slice on broiled fish or on a lemon mousse.
Twisted lime slices go well with raw fish dishes or on melon wedges.
Top off roast duckling, broiled chicken or an orange tart
with a twisted orange slice.

VARIATIONS

■ For a contrasting yellow-and-red effect, cut a lemon slice from the center to the edge and pat half the surface of one side on a plate of paprika before twisting the halves forward and backward.

■ For a contrasting orange-and-green effect, cut an orange slice from the center to the edge and pat half the surface of one side on a plate of finely minced parsley before twisting the halves forward and backward.

■ To make a colored stripe across the center of the citrus slice, hold 2 edges of the slice up, and dip the center of the slice onto a plate of paprika or finely minced parsley. Use the slice flat rather than slitting and twisting it.

■ Use a lemon stripper to score lengthwise the rind of citrus fruit or skin of a cucumber before slicing. Each slice will then have a notched edge.

■ Cucumber twists: Float a twisted cucumber slice on cucumber soup or decorate the perimeter of a salad bowl with several cucumber twists.

■ Radish twists: Decorate a cold cut platter or a salad plate with twisted radish slices.

FANCY TOAST

Cut toasted bread into triangles or slender sticks.

Dip the points of the triangles or the ends of the sticks
into the sauce or gravy to be used with the dish, then dip

them into finely minced parsley.

Place the toast around
the edge of beef stew, coq au vin or seafood Newburg.

MINISKEWERS

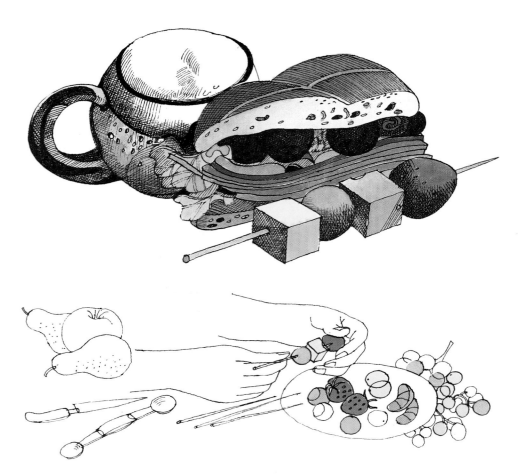

Simple sandwich platters can be highlighted with interesting shapes and colors by combining fruits, vegetables and cheese on decorative picks. Select foods with tastes that combine well with the dish and with each other. Use small ingredients such as grapes and mushrooms in their natural shapes. Cut others into wedges, cubes or balls.

   Try the combination of a pineapple chunk, a mandarin orange section and a red or green grape. Skewer a strawberry, a melon ball and an apple wedge onto a pick. A piece of baby zucchini, cherry tomato and a small mushroom cap make a pleasing trio, as do a chunk of raw turnip, a carrot ball and a small piece of celery. To combine fruit and cheese, try a cube of cheddar cheese, a pear wedge and a cube of Swiss cheese.

BUTTERFLIES

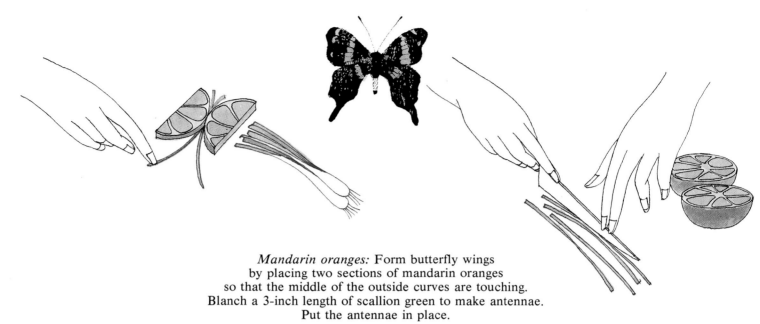

Mandarin oranges: Form butterfly wings
by placing two sections of mandarin oranges
so that the middle of the outside curves are touching.
Blanch a 3-inch length of scallion green to make antennae.
Put the antennae in place.

Tomato or peach wedges: Cut a fresh tomato half or a peach half (canned or fresh) into wedges and position them as butterfly wings. Use blanched scallion green for antennae. Serve tomato butterflies with cold-cut platters or pasta salad.

Pineapple slices: Cut a fresh or canned pineapple ring into halves. Position them as butterfly wings and add blanched scallion green as antennae. Use with cottage cheese salad or on slices of baked ham (in which case, add the antennae after baking is completed).

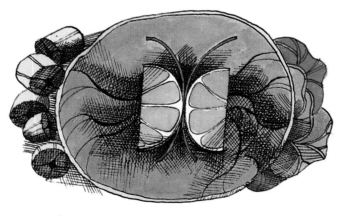

Serve the butterflies on salad or meat dishes.

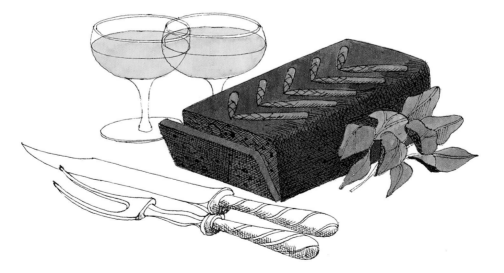

Long slender vegetables such as cooked asparagus
or cooked green beans can be arranged in a decorative
herringbone design on a background of meat, a vegetable
terrine or a ham steak. Use 2 asparagus or green beans
to form an angle. Use 2 more pieces of vegetable to
form the same angle, just inside the first one. Continue,
using as many pairs of asparagus or green beans as you
wish to serve.

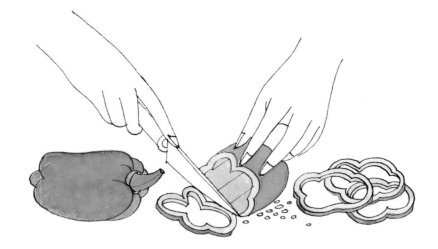

Raw red or white onions, or red or green peppers can be
sliced into rings and used as decorative toppings on
casseroles or salads. Cluster overlapping separate rings in
the center of the serving arrangement.

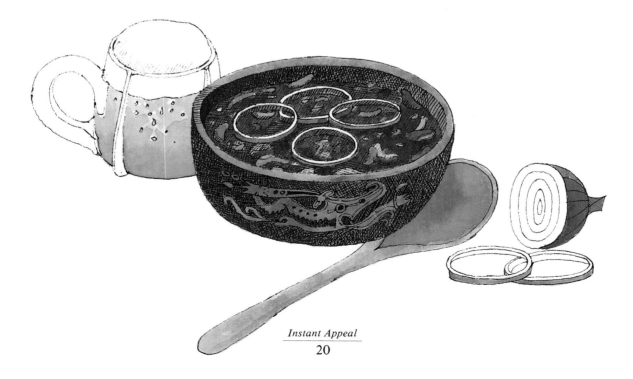

Instant Appeal

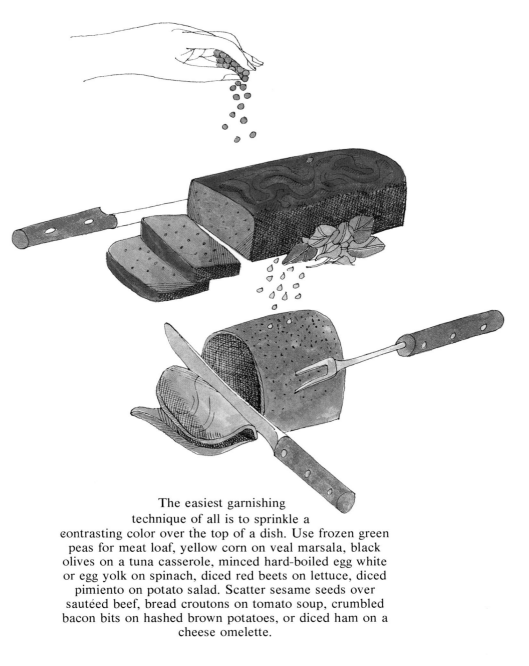

The easiest garnishing
technique of all is to sprinkle a
contrasting color over the top of a dish. Use frozen green
peas for meat loaf, yellow corn on veal marsala, black
olives on a tuna casserole, minced hard-boiled egg white
or egg yolk on spinach, diced red beets on lettuce, diced
pimiento on potato salad. Scatter sesame seeds over
sautéed beef, bread croutons on tomato soup, crumbled
bacon bits on hashed brown potatoes, or diced ham on a
cheese omelette.

NATURAL CONTAINERS

Make natural edible containers to present sauces, dips, salads or ice cream. Large mushroom caps or artichoke bottoms can hold individual servings of sauce for meats or hold dressings for salads. Slice off the tops of tomatoes or peppers, hollow out the vegetables and fill them with vegetable dip for appetizers. Gently roll back the outer leaves of a red or white cabbage, cut away the inside leaves and use the center as a bowl for a vegetable dip. Use a fresh avocado, cut in half, and pitted, as a container for seafood salad. Use pear or peach halves to hold a scoop of cottage cheese or a scoop of ice cream.

The easy-to-follow procedures in this chapter unravel the mysteries of seemingly complicated professional garnishes. Tie vegetables into little bundles, encircle cheese sticks with fruit rings, scoop salads into citrus baskets, arrange sandwiches in a hollowed loaf of bread.

Once you learn any one technique, you can create several different garnishes by varying the method or applying it to different ingredients.

TIED BUNDLES AND PACKAGES

Magically, the sight of small gift packages imparts an extra joy to special occasions. These tiny bundles of vegetables tied with an edible ribbon are particularly fun to serve at a birthday or anniversary meal as an accompaniment to roast meats, grilled chops or poached fish.

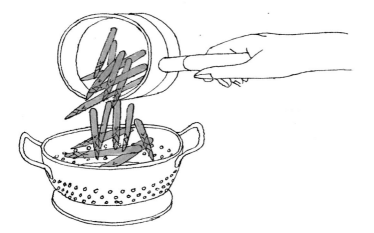
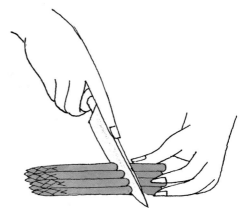

Asparagus bundles: Rinse slender, fresh green or white asparagus to remove any sand. Cook them in simmering water until tender. Rinse immediately with cold water; drain; dry.

Arrange the stalks so that all the tips are even. Trim to an equal length (2 to 2½ inches).

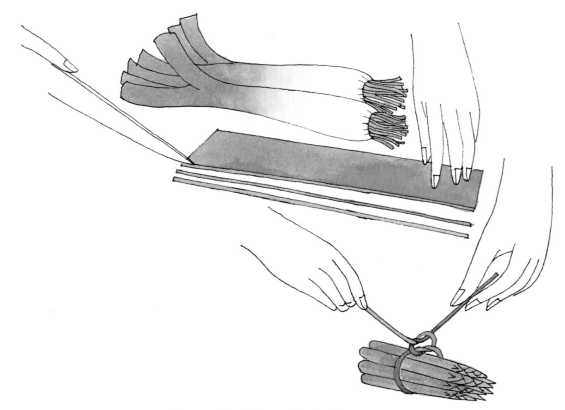

Prepare the ribbon of leek strip:
Cut and rinse a 7-inch piece of leek green.
Blanch it in boiling water for 10 seconds and rinse
in cold water. Lay it flat on a cutting board;
lengthwise, cut a 1/4-inch-wide strip. You can make
several leek strips from one piece of leek green.

Tie the leek strip into a bow around each portion of
asparagus. Serve one bundle per portion.

VARIATIONS

■ Substitute canned asparagus spears. Do not blanch or cook the spears; simply heat them and tie them into bundles with a bow.

■ Tie portions of cooked green beans, or julienne strips of cooked carrots, celery or beets into bundles.

Tied Bundles and Packages

RINGS AROUND THINGS

A simple ring encircling stalks of vegetables or sticks of cheese makes a plate look well dressed, and shows that it has received more care than mere chance.

Rings of fruit or uncooked vegetables go well on sandwich platters; rings of cooked vegetables are nice accompaniments to hot meat or poultry dishes.

Apple rings: Cut an apple into 1/4-inch slices. An average-size apple will yield 6 to 8 rings.

Cut each slice into a ring, using a fluted or round circle cutter, and a smaller plain round cutter. Dip the rings of fruits into lemon juice or acidulated water to keep them white.

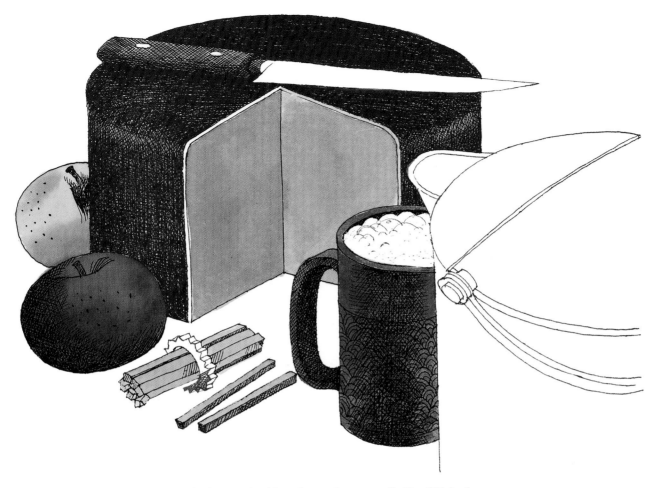

Cut Swiss or cheddar cheese into pencil-slim 2½-inch-
long sticks. Place a portion of cheese sticks through the
center of each apple ring.

VARIATIONS

■ Pear rings: Cut 1/4-inch slices from the large section
of pears. Use 2 cutters of different sizes to cut a ring
from each slice. Dip the rings into lemon juice. Place
cheese sticks through the centers.
■ Zucchini rings: Leave the skin on and cut only the
inside circle to form a ring. Sauté or steam the rings

briefly and allow to cool. Place cooked green or yellow
string beans through the center of the rings.
■ Peel a medium-size red or white onion, slice it into
rings and slip them around celery or carrot stalks.
■ Slice a small red or green pepper, remove the seeds
and use the rings to encircle raw vegetable sticks.

BASKETS WITHOUT HANDLES

Plain fruit and vegetable baskets are not only attractive, but versatile and particularly economical, because you can make two identical baskets from a single whole piece. Their open shape is also practical because guests can eat from them easily. Fluting the edge with diagonal zigzag cuts makes the basket look festive. The secret to the most beautiful baskets is to make each cut uniformly deep and wide.

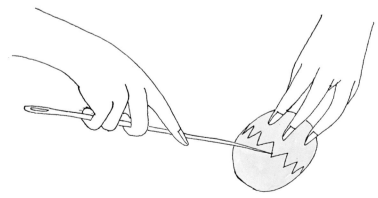

Lemon baskets: Trim the top and bottom of a lemon to form a stable base at both ends. Mark an imaginary, or light pencil line around the middle.

Cut zigzags or curves back and forth across the line, being sure to cut all the way into the center of the fruit.

Adjust the last cut around the middle to meet the first cut. Separate the halves. Place half a purple grape in the center of each half. Serve with fish or poultry dishes requiring lemon juice.

VARIATIONS

■ Make other citrus baskets using limes, oranges or grapefruits. Orange and lime baskets go well with poultry and fish dishes. Serve grapefruit baskets as a first course or to perk up breakfast.
■ Honeydew and cantaloupe baskets (seeds removed, of course) are delicious served on their own or filled with ice cream or mixed fruit.

■ Fill hollowed tomato baskets with spinach puree, green peas or broccoli florets.
■ To make a green pepper basket, cut off the top using a zigzag or wavy curved design. Save the top to dice and sprinkle over a salad. Remove the ribs and seeds and fill with macaroni or potato salad. Each pepper makes one basket.

SINGLE-HANDLED BASKETS

Single-handled baskets add extra height that enhances dishes that would otherwise appear flat and two-dimensional on the plate. Try to make them perfectly upright by trimming the base.

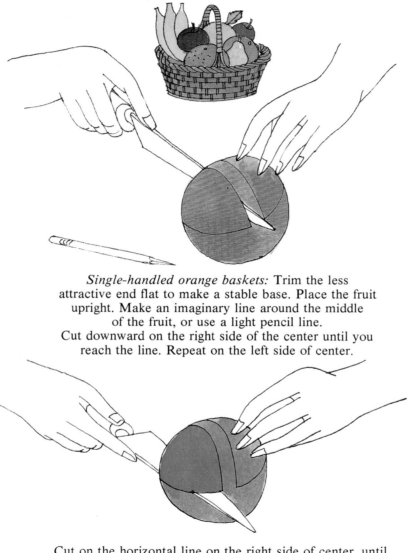

Single-handled orange baskets: Trim the less attractive end flat to make a stable base. Place the fruit upright. Make an imaginary line around the middle of the fruit, or use a light pencil line.
Cut downward on the right side of the center until you reach the line. Repeat on the left side of center.

Cut on the horizontal line on the right side of center, until you reach the right side vertical cut.
Repeat on the left side.

For an added touch, make a basket-weave design on the rind. Remove the pulp with a grapefruit knife.

VARIATIONS

■ Fill grapefruit baskets with assorted fruit and serve as a first course or dessert.

■ Lemon or lime baskets need not be hollowed; serve them with foods that call for fresh juice.

■ Cherry tomato baskets can be filled with softened cream cheese piped from a pastry bag fitted with a small tip. Omit the basket-weave design on the skin. Serve as an hors d'oeuvre.

With its delicately curved handles tied together with a pretty bow, this basket is well suited to elegant presentations. Grapefruit baskets are large enough to hold generous servings of fresh fruit salad. If you make the baskets from lemons, limes or oranges, serve them with main courses of fish or poultry either to be squeezed over the food or filled with tartar sauce or relish.

Prepare a ribbon of leek strip: Cut and rinse a 7-inch piece of leek green. Blanch it in boiling water for 10 seconds; rinse it in cold water. Lay it flat on a cutting board and cut a 1/4-inch-wide strip lengthwise. You can make several leek strips from one leek green.

Double-handled grapefruit baskets: Cut the fruit in half horizontally. Trim a flat base on each half. Mark 1/2-inch segments at 2 opposite points of each top surface. These segments are to remain uncut.

Leaving the pulp and rind intact at those segments, slice horizontally 1/4 inch below the cut edge. Use a grapefruit knife to remove all the pulp.

Gently lift the 2 opposite sides of the rind to form handles. Tie them together with a bow made of a leek strip.

Double-Handled Baskets

SHALLOW CONTAINERS

A shallow container is simply a hollowed-out base that holds a small amount of food to complement the main ingredient of the dish. It raises a mere spoonful of relish to majestic standing. Serve alongside sandwich platters or with hot entrees.

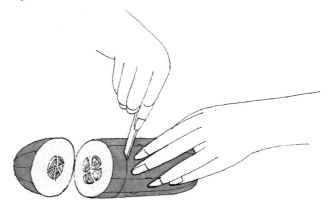

Shallow cucumber containers: Select a cucumber with a large diameter. Cut it crosswise into 3/4-inch slices.

Cut each slice with a fluted round cutter with a diameter slightly smaller than the diameter of the cucumber.

Hollow out a bowl in the center of each slice of cucumber
with a melon scoop. Fill it with corn relish or other
relish, place mint or basil leaves on each side of the
shallow container to set it off.

VARIATIONS

■ A shallow container of cooked squash can hold cranberry relish, a vegetable puree or applesauce.

■ Cooked zucchini containers are attractive filled with cooked corn or stewed tomatoes.

■ Turnips make a good base for tiny green peas or carrot puree.

Deep containers make an impressive presentation and can hold a variety of ingredients.

The secret to hollowing a deep container is the nearly invisible slit made near the bottom. Use a knife with a narrow blade, such as a boning knife or a ham slicer, to make the narrowest possible slit.

Fill a pineapple with fruit or chicken pineapple salad with macadamia nuts, or fill it with sherbet and freeze it until serving time. Replace the cover before serving.

Hollow out a large round loaf of peasant bread and use the "core" of bread to make assorted tea sandwiches; serve them arranged in the loaf.

Deep pineapple containers: Trim the bottom to form a stable base. Cut off the top about 1 inch below the leaves and set it aside.

Insert the tip of a long knife into the pineapple about 1/2 inch from the outside edge. Push the knife down into the fruit until the tip is 1/2 inch from the bottom. Cut around the pineapple in a circle.

Insert the knife, blade flat, into the side of the pineapple, 1/2 inch from the base. Pivot the flat knife back and forth to release the flesh. Lift out the fruit and core in a single piece.

KNOTS

Although these delicate and intriguing knots may look intricate, they are easily made with a few simple slices and twists. They are as light as a feather and add variety and dimension to presentations.

Knots made of raw carrots are excellent mixed in cold pasta salads. Create the same knot with noodle dough and deep-fry it; it makes a wonderful snack sprinkled with coarse salt or confectioners' sugar.

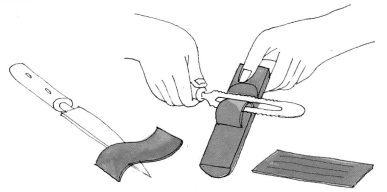

Carrot knots: Select a carrot about 1¼ inches in diameter. Peel and cut it in half lengthwise. Make 3-inch-long strips from the cut sides with a vegetable peeler.

Cut 3 parallel 1-inch slits lengthwise in each carrot strip.

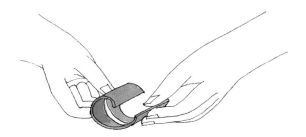

Tuck one end of the strip through the center slit. Gently pull it through as far as it will go.

The other two slits will twist on their own. Repeat with
the remaining slits. Crisp the twists by placing them
in a bowl of ice water for a few hours or overnight.

VARIATION

■ Cut squares of wonton wrappers in half, to form 2 rectangles, 3 inches by 1½ inches. In each rectangle, cut 3 parallel 1-inch slits and twist as for carrot knots. Deep-fry the noodle knots; drain, sprinkle with coarse salt as a snack or to accompany a savory dish. Sprinkle with confectioners' sugar, to serve like a cookie.

Slice. Slice thin. That's all there is to making these delicate garnishes. It is quick to do, inexpensive, and no exotic ingredients are needed!

Fans and sprays made of cucumbers are a classic Chinese garnish on appetizer platters. Fans of gherkins or cornichons traditionally accompany French pates. Baby eggplant or zucchini can be cut into fans, breaded and deep-fried, maintaining their pretty outspread shape. Serve them as a side dish.

Cucumber fans: Choose a large straight cucumber. Cut a slice lengthwise from the side of the cucumber. The slice should be about 1/2-inch thick at the thickest part.

Place the cucumber slice cut side down on a cutting board and trim off the far right tip at a 45-degree angle.

Select a thin-bladed knife, such as a fish fillet knife. Leaving the top 1/4-inch edge uncut, start on the right-hand end of the cucumber and cut about 8 thin parallel slices, 1/16-inch wide, then cut off the section. Cut another 8 or so parallel cuts, and cut off a second section. Repeat to make as many fans as you wish. With just one cucumber you can make dozens of fans!

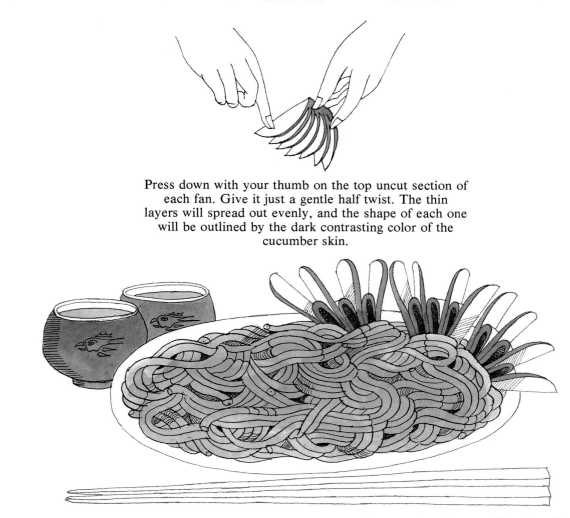

Press down with your thumb on the top uncut section of each fan. Give it just a gentle half twist. The thin layers will spread out evenly, and the shape of each one will be outlined by the dark contrasting color of the cucumber skin.

Cucumber sprays: Make lots of cucumber sprays to scatter or to cluster on presentation platters or individual plates. These start out being made like the cucumber fans, but have a fancy step added. Make each section of only 3, 5 or 7 slices. Make loops with the second, fourth and sixth cucumber slices, tucking them in toward the uncut edge. Place the cucumber sprays in a bowl of ice water for several hours or overnight to set the shape. Arrange on platters of sliced meats and cheeses, or float on chilled summertime soups.

VARIATIONS

■ Gherkins or tiny pickles can be fanned by slicing them lengthwise into 6 or 8 layers.
■ Slice baby eggplant or zucchini lengthwise in 1/2-inch slices, fan them out as you would the cucumber, lightly bread them and deep-fry them. Season with salt and pepper.

Jagged-edge wisps are easily made using to decorative advantage the curling effect that cold water has on vegetables. Float a few light airy spinach or celery wisps in the center of a bowl of soup as a focal point. Beet wisps curling curiously out of a fresh beet make an interesting garnish for a serving tray. Several beets grouped together make a fascinating centerpiece. Be careful to protect the table linens from beet stains.

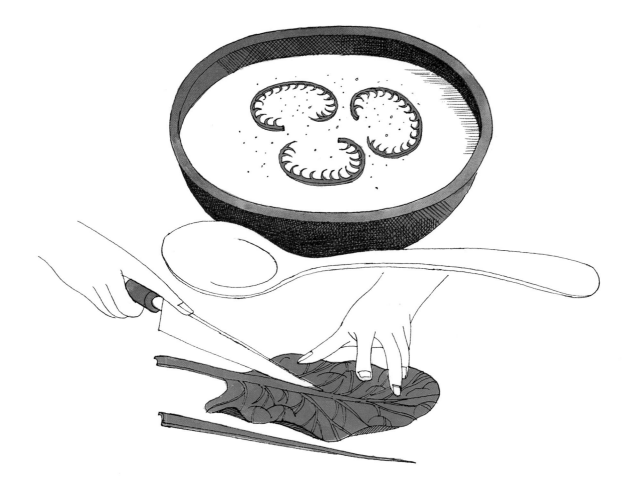

Spinach wisps: Trim the stems from spinach leaves.

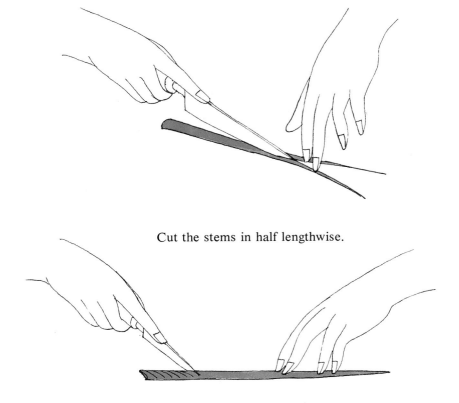

Cut the stems in half lengthwise.

Make short, angular parallel cuts at regularly spaced
intervals along one edge of each strip.
Be careful to keep the strips
whole. Soak the strips in cold water for a few hours;
they will curl, forming shaggy decorative wisps.

VARIATIONS

■ Make celery wisps by splitting a stalk of celery into very thin strips. Make short, angular parallel cuts at regularly spaced intervals along one edge of each strip. Soak the strips in cold water until they curl.

■ Trim a flat base on a fresh beet, leaving the stems attached. Trim the leaves from the stems, and trim the stems to about 6 inches long. Split thick stems in half or thirds to make slender strips. Make short, angular parallel cuts along one edge of each strip. Soak the beet upside down in cold water for several hours until the strips curl.

The cumulative effect of concentric wedges is greater than the sum of the parts. This sophisticated look belies how easy it is to create.

Use each set of wedges separately, or cluster several together. Concentric fruit or vegetable wedges are appropriate served with either hot or cold foods at any course of a meal, and are especially nice arranged on a cheese tray.

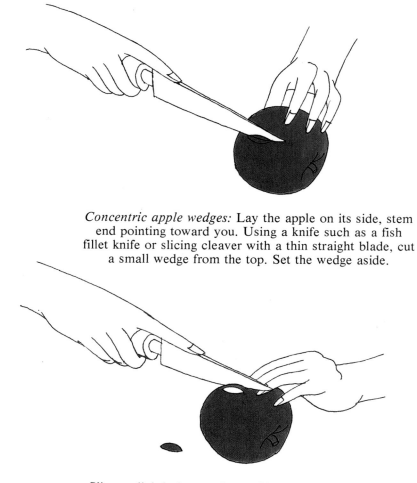

Concentric apple wedges: Lay the apple on its side, stem end pointing toward you. Using a knife such as a fish fillet knife or slicing cleaver with a thin straight blade, cut a small wedge from the top. Set the wedge aside.

Slice a slightly larger, deeper V-shaped wedge from the ' same place. Set the wedge aside also.
Continue slicing consecutively larger, deeper pieces until 4 to 6 pieces are cut. Dip the pieces in lemon juice to keep them white.

Reassemble the pieces in their original order. Shingle, or spread the pieces to highlight their outlines and form a repeated design. You can make 3 or 4 sets of concentric wedges from a single apple.

VARIATIONS

■ Combine sets of red, green and yellow concentric apple wedges for extra color.

■ Radishes, black olives, tomatoes, green peppers, cantaloupe and pears all make attractive wedges.

GELATIN WEDGES

Youngsters enjoy the sweetness of flavored gelatin, especially when it is served in wedges with a rim of contrasting color. For adults, gelatin wedges add interest in both texture and color to turkey dinners and cold meat platters, particularly when filled with homemade jellied cranberry sauce or mint jelly. Try to select evenly shaped fruits with thick rinds. Don't limit yourself to just one fruit, try lemon and lime rinds for variety.

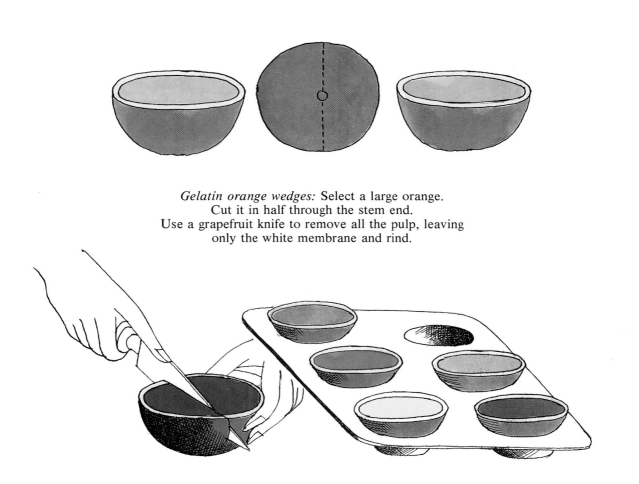

Gelatin orange wedges: Select a large orange.
Cut it in half through the stem end.
Use a grapefruit knife to remove all the pulp, leaving
only the white membrane and rind.

To hold the bowl-shaped orange rinds upright, place them
on top of muffin-tin cups. Fill each orange rind
to the top with colored, flavored gelatin. Use red, yellow,
green or orange, depending on what main course
you are serving. Chill for several hours or overnight
to set the gelatin.

Heat a knife blade with hot water, wipe the
blade dry, and quickly slice each orange half into
2 or 3 equal-sized wedges. Keep chilled until serving.

The principle of carving a cylindrical vegetable into a decorative shape, and slicing it into multiple garnishes, is the same as making a roll of refrigerator cookies and slicing it into individual cookies. Take care in shaping the vegetable, then simply cut one slice after another, forming a generous heap!

Use the decorative shapes raw in salads or cook them briefly to add to cooked foods. Scatter the shapes generously in a background of pasta primavera, rice pilaf, soup or stew. These small designs perk up the routine combination of carrots and peas to make it an attractive and appetizing side dish.

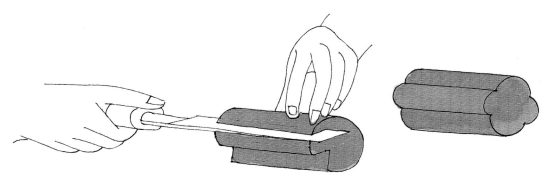

Carve-and-slice carrot flowers: Select a large carrot (at least 3/4 inch in diameter). Use only the thick end. Peel the carrot with a vegetable peeler and form an even cylinder by trimming away any irregularities. Blanch the carrot briefly in boiling water; immediately rinse it in cold water and dry.

Using a knife with a thin and straight blade, such as a thin slicing cleaver, carve 4 equally spaced notches lengthwise in the carrot. Round out each notch to form rounded petals.

Slice into 1/8-inch-thick flowers.

VARIATIONS

■ Four-petal flowers are the fastest to make, but with a bit of patience you can make 6-petal flowers, too. This is one of the garnishes most adaptable to special occasions. Choose distinctive silhouettes such as heart shapes for Valentine's Day dinner, or heart, spade, diamond and club shapes for a card party meal. Make apple shapes for a back-to-school event, umbrella shapes for a bridal shower and pipe or top-hat shapes for a Father's Day dinner.

■ Trim broccoli stalks to a cylindrical shape, blanch the cylinder and then carve shapes from the broccoli as you would from a carrot. Slice the carved cylinder as above.

SAWTOOTH THREADS

Garnishes can be neat and compact, but they can also be as long and willowy as the longest carrot. Place 3 or 4 carrot threads on a bed of sauce to create a perfect background for a fish fillet or a slice of meat. These threads create design interest in an otherwise plain plate presentation, and can be used sparingly or generously.

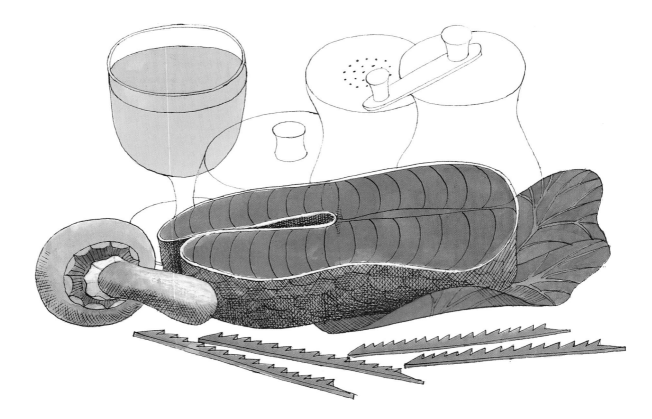

Sawtooth carrot threads: Select a slender carrot. Peel it and cut it in half lengthwise. Place it on a cutting board, cut surface down, thick end on the right.

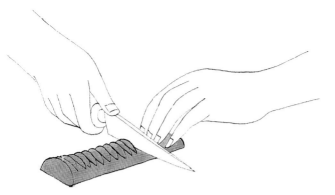

Select a knife with a thin and straight edge, such as a thin slicing cleaver. Starting at the right tip, make alternate cuts straight down, 1/8 inch to 1/4 inch deep and then at 45-degree angles to that cut, removing a small wedge with every 2 cuts. The carrot top surface will then look jagged or saw-toothed.
Repeat with the other half of the carrot.

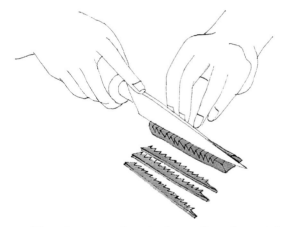

Slice the carrot lengthwise to form long strips with 1 straight edge and 1 sawtooth edge. Trim the straight edge close to the jagged edge to make a narrower strip.

VARIATION

■ Long white turnip threads can be placed in pale-colored sauces on plates of meats and fish.

FLUTED MUSHROOM CAPS

Few garnishes are more classic in Continental cuisine than fluted, or turned, mushroom caps. You may find it takes a couple of baskets of mushrooms to master the technique, but keep at it. Practice does make perfect! The secret is to relax. A tense hand cannot flute a mushroom as smoothly as a relaxed one. Nothing need be wasted, however; use any scraps you make practicing in omelettes, quiches, stuffing, soups or stews. Elegantly turned mushrooms are a fine highlight for steak, chicken or fish entrees.

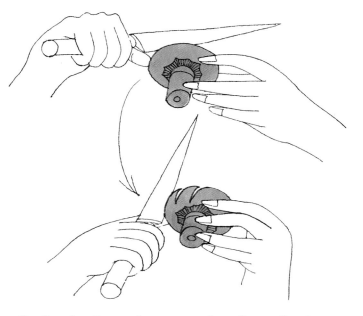

Gently wipe the mushroom cap clean. Leave the stem on.
Hold the mushroom in your left hand.
Hold a paring knife with the blade at a 45-degree angle
to the top of the cap, blade pointed away from you.
With right wrist and elbow up,
rest the thumb of your right hand directly in front of you,
on the mushroom cap.

Use your thumb as a pivot point. Do not rock your wrist
back and forth. As you pivot your hand downward
like the hand of a clock, a sliver of mushroom will be
lifted from the cap.

Turn the mushroom cap with your left hand.
Reposition the knife and your thumb. Repeat until you
have flutes all the way around the cap. Remove the stem.

Sauté the caps in butter, adding a few drops of lemon
juice to help keep them light-colored.

Fluted Mushroom Caps

BACKGROUND GARNISH

When greens such as spinach are deep-fried, they curiously resemble seaweed, which makes them intriguing background for presenting seafood, particularly deep-fried shrimp, clams, oysters and fish. A pinch of deep-fried spinach, parsley or broccoli leaves makes a dark fluffy contrast on top of baked potatoes.

Deep-fried spinach background: Remove tough stems from 1 pound fresh spinach leaves. Rinse the leaves and dry them thoroughly. Any remaining water will cause the cooking oil to spatter.

Shred the spinach into 1/8-inch-wide strips.

Fill a deep 4-quart pot or a deep-fryer with 2½ inches of vegetable oil. Heat the oil to 350 degrees Fahrenheit. Gradually add a handful of shredded spinach. (Add no more than one handful because the oil level will rise, and if you add too much spinach at a time, the oil could overflow.) Fry the spinach for about 2 minutes until it is dark green and crispy. Lift the spinach out with a slotted spoon and drain on paper towels. Continue cooking a handful of spinach at a time until all the spinach is cooked.

Flowers such as chrysanthemums, roses and daisies can be made from edible materials. They may be used as single blossoms or small nosegays, and combined to make colorful and appetizing bouquets.

You can make different styles of flowers using techniques of crisscross cutting, slicing, carving, feathering, and by using scissors and shaped cutters. These versatile methods can be applied to different fruits and vegetables to make a wide variety of flowers.

Some of the flowers suggested here are intended to be eaten with the food they accompany. Others are more appropriate for decorating serving plates and buffet tables.

FLOWERS MADE WITH PEELS AND SKINS

The outside of the fruit or vegetable, the part you usually throw away, can make a most graceful rose. Although it looks intricate, it is easy to learn how to make roses. Place the flower on a serving plate of meat or poultry.

Add a leaf of basil or mint to set off the rose's color. Make flowers of apple, orange, lemon or lime using the same techniques. Use on serving platters of cheese, meat, poultry or fish, respectively.

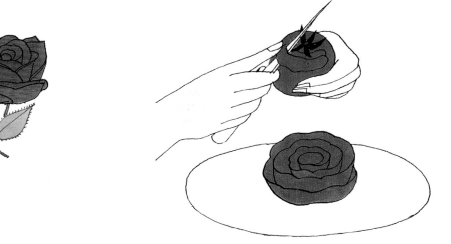

Tomato rose: Starting at either the top or bottom of the tomato, use a paring knife to remove the skin in one long continuous strip about 3/4 inch wide.

Rewind the skin in a coil. Avoid rolling the peel up into a flat roll like a roll of postage stamps. Start out with a fairly tight turn, and let each successive turn fan out slightly more. Sometimes the rose is more attractive turned upside down. Tip it into your other hand to see!

FLOWERS MADE BY
CRISSCROSS CUTTING

A multitude of little petals can be formed by cutting vegetables in a crisscross pattern. As they open, they become full and rounded flower blossoms. Decorate trays of savory appetizers or roast meat with onion chrysanthemums. Radishes cut this way are colorful clustered in a salad or an arrangement of crudites.

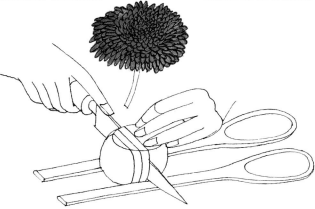

Onion chrysanthemum: Select an onion
that is evenly formed, having no side or inner bulbs.
Slice off the top and peel the onion, leaving
the root end intact.

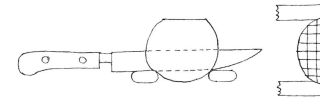

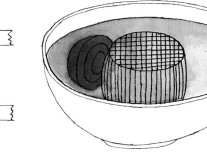

Place flat wooden spatulas or long pencils on 2 opposite sides of the onion. Cut perpendicular to the wooden spatulas, starting about 1/2 inch from one edge; cut across at 1/8-inch intervals, stopping 1/2 inch from the opposite edge. The wooden spatulas should keep you from cutting all the way through.

Rotate the onion 90 degrees. Repeat cutting across, in the same way, perpendicular to the first set of cuts. Gently place the cut onion in a bowl of ice water and let it soak for an hour until the petals open.
To color the flower a delicate pink, put a freshly cut beet in the bowl of water when soaking the onion.

Using the following simple techniques, one tomato yields three tulips! These flowers are not only decorative, but are clearly intended to be eaten. Serve them with salads or main courses of poultry, seafood or meat. Tulips made with oranges may be served with main courses or desserts.

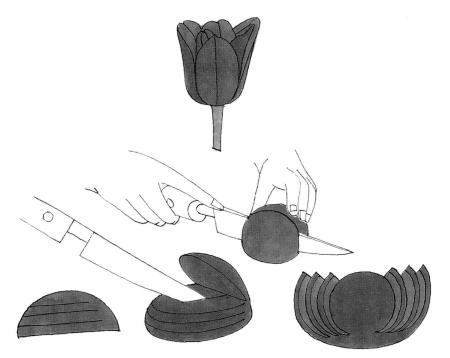

Tomato tulips: Slice off one-third of a tomato, cutting across one face of the vegetable.

Lay the piece on a cutting board, cut side down. Make 3 parallel horizontal slices, leaving the part toward the tomato stem uncut.

Lift the top slice. Insert the tip of the knife under the section and slice the 3 lower sections in half with a downward cut. Fan apart the lower sections slightly to resemble the petals of a tulip.

Even the least artistic sculptor can work a flower from the end of a carrot stick or icicle turnip. Small buttercups are dainty flowers to use in an edible flower arrangement.

Larger flowers can be cut from cucumbers or zucchini and clustered on serving platters. These larger flower cups can also be hollowed out to hold dipping sauces.

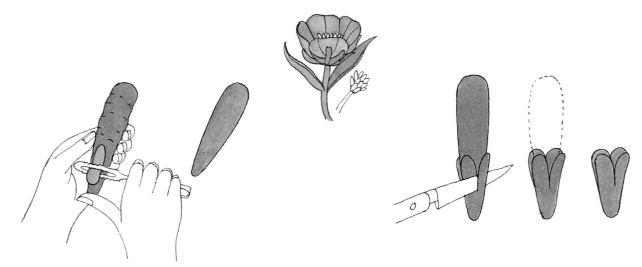

Carrot buttercups: Use a vegetable peeler or a knife to peel a carrot and shape the tip to a delicately tapered cup.

Cut one petal, starting about 1 inch from the tip and peeling down toward the tip, but do not cut the petal off. Continue cutting petals all the way around the tip.

Gently twist the remaining top of the carrot to remove it from the newly formed flower cup. Reshape the tip and repeat cutting flowers from the remaining carrot, until you use the entire carrot stick. Use the buttercup flowers as they are, or add a contrasting center such as a small piece of zucchini, radish or turnip. Secure the center with a dab of gelatin. If you use the flowers for decoration only, use a toothpick to help keep the center in place.

VARIATIONS

■ Shape an icicle radish to a tapered point and cut flowers from it.

■ On a larger scale, shape unpeeled cucumbers or zucchini to a point. First trim the end of a cucumber or zucchini flat to make a base. Then starting 2 to 3 inches from the base, cut a petal downward toward the center of the vegetable. Rotate the vegetable to form 3 or 4 similar petals. Twist the flower off, and continue to shape more flower cups with the remaining part of the vegetable. Place an olive or red grape in the center for contrast, or use a melon baller to scoop out the pulp and fill the flower cup with an appetizer sauce.

FLOWERS MADE BY FEATHERING

Flowers made by feathering are soft and gentle-looking. They can be large, made with leeks, or small, made with scallions. Either way, they are very simple to create. Leek flowers are attractive on serving trays of hors d'oeuvres and canapes. Smaller scallion flowers look nice both in salad arrangements and on individual plates.

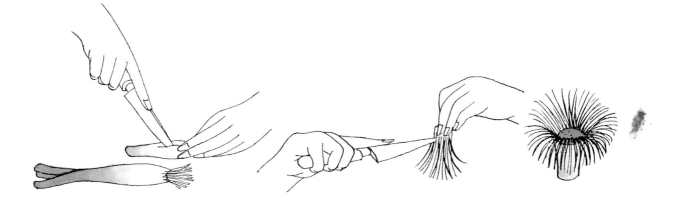

Leek spider mum: Trim off the root of a leek. Cut a
3-inch section of leek white.

With the tip of a paring knife,
cut 2-inch-long parallel slits lengthwise in the leek white, leaving
1 inch at the root end uncut. Cut all the way through
to the center layers. Cut as many parallel slits as will fit
in the leek, to make the fluffiest flower.

Soak the cut leek in ice water for several hours until the
featured ends curl. Leave in the water until you are ready
to serve. Cut a slender stick of carrot to poke into the
center for a contrast of colors. If the flower is for
decoration only, use a toothpick to secure half a carrot
ball in the flower center.

VARIATIONS

■ Scallion flowers are made in exactly the same way and take only a few minutes in ice water to curl.

■ To make a decorative brush, with 2 fluffy ends, feather a scallion on each end, leaving the center third uncut.

Take advantage of the interesting seed design inside peppers. Cut the outside into slender petals that curl open, and leave the cluster of seeds in place. Pepper lilies, cut from red, green and yellow peppers, are colorful additions to flower arrangements.

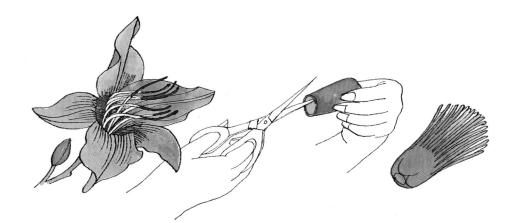

Pepper lilies: Select small, thin peppers about 2 inches long. Cut off the tip so that only 1½ inches remains at the stem end.

Using a pair of small sharp scissors, cut 1-inch-long by 1/8-inch-wide parallel strips all around the pepper, leaving the strips attached to the stem end.

Soak the flower in a bowl of ice water for an hour, or until the petals curl open.

VARIATIONS

■ Cut petals 1/2 inch wide, and use scissors to round the edges. Soak in ice water. The flower will look quite different with wider, rounded petals.

■ Use longer skinny peppers, cutting them in half and making a flower from each end of the pepper. One flower may have seeds while the other may not, but both will curl.

FLOWERS MADE USING PRESHAPED CUTTERS

When you want a lot of flowers, make these neat and crisp-looking daisies. They are easy and fast to mass produce. The blossoms alone are pretty to scatter in a relish tray or a basket of vegetables with dip. The flowers also make lovely additions to vegetable flower arrangements.

Use colored turnips and squash to make subtly different flowers; use white radish balls as centers.

Daisies: Cut a raw, unpeeled rutabaga turnip into 3/8-inch slices. An electric meat-slicing machine is useful if you are cutting a large quantity of turnips.

Use a flower-shaped cutter to cut the shapes. If you cut several flowers, one after another, your hand may get sore from repeatedly pressing on the metal cutter. To protect your hand, place a flat wooden spoon over the cutter and press down on the spoon instead of directly on the cutter. This way you can easily cut as many flowers as you like.

Use a melon baller to cut a ball of raw carrot. Trim each ball so you have just half a ball. Secure the half ball of carrot to the center of each flower, using a dab of unflavored gelatin as glue. If the flowers are to be used for decoration only, secure each flower center with a concealed toothpick, cutting off any excess length.

You can make a grand bouquet for a dining table centerpiece with daisies made of turnips, chrysanthemums made of leeks and radishes, buttercups carved from carrots, and lilies cut from small peppers. Equally delightful is a single flower or two on a small base. Such a simple touch adds cheer to a tray for breakfast in bed, or a simple lunch for one.

Any flower that can be supported on a skewer stem is suitable for a vase arrangement. (Avoid flowers that need a flat surface to keep them intact, such as the tomato-skin rose, tomato tulip and onion chrysanthemum. Use these flowers directly on a plate or tray.)

Make the flowers using the various techniques previously described. To arrange them on a stem and in a vase takes just a couple of easy steps.

Choose one type of flower, or combine them as you like. Put the flowers into the vase or base, paying attention to the scale of the arrangement, the direction the flowers face and the overall composition, just as you would with real flowers. Then fill in the arrangement with leaves made from leek greens or curly-leafed vegetables.

Keep the arrangement fresh by spraying it with a mist of water. If you make it a day ahead, keep it in the refrigerator, covered with a plastic bag.

Vases and bases: Use vegetables with well-balanced shapes such as eggplant and squash for simple vases. Trim a piece from the bottom to form a stable base for the vase. Trim the top to make a surface for inserting the flower stems. You might like to use a lemon stripper to etch a free-form design on the vegetable vase before arranging the flowers in it.

Instead of using vegetable vases, you could hold the flowers upright by sticking them into a base such as half an unpeeled potato, or half a cabbage, cut surface down. If you use just one or two flowers at a time, they look charming placed in a section of zucchini or cucumber. Just cut a 2-inch section in half lengthwise, place the cut side down and insert the flowers.

Stems: Cut a wooden skewer to the length you want the stem to be, plus at least 1½ inches for inserting the stem into the vase or base. Slip a scallion green over the skewer. Pierce the pointed end of the skewer into the flower blossom, at an angle. Let the scallion come up far enough to visually soften the joining of the flower and the stem. Insert the flowers one by one into the vase or base.

Leaves and green filler: To make long bold leaves, wash raw leek leaves and cut them into slightly tapered leaf shapes. Tuck them among the flowers and hold them in place by anchoring them with toothpicks. Conceal the picks and visually soften the area where the stems join the vase by tucking in raw leafy greens such as carrot tops, spinach or curly parsley.

Techniques for Making Flowers

What better reason to make garnishes than because they are just plain fun to make and serve! These friendly animals of land, sea and air add extra charm to almost any meal. They are the ultimate in fanciful garnishes and will display the culmination of your versatile techniques.

TURTLE

Cute little turtles are amusing to carve from cucumbers and are especially loved by youngsters. Garnish a sandwich, or a bowl of hot soup—not necessarily turtle soup—with a single turtle or a scattering of them. When making the turtles, let the natural curve of cucumbers help shape the animal bodies.

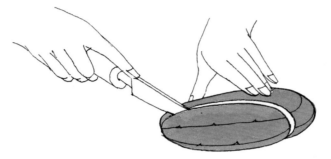

Select a straight cucumber. Cut a slice lengthwise from one side. The slice should be about 1/2 inch thick at the thickest part. Place it on a cutting board, with the cut surface down.

Make a paper pattern by drawing and cutting out the silhouette of a turtle, as shown.

Place the paper pattern on the cucumber, picking a place that is dark-colored and curved to suit the turtle's shell. Use the sharp, flat tip of a trussing needle or a paring knife to draw the outline of a turtle on the cucumber. Cut along the outline, using the tip of the trussing needle or paring knife.

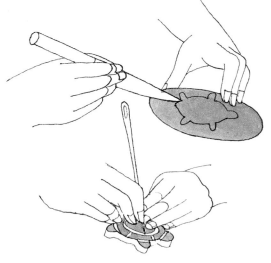

Remove the cucumber skin from the head, feet and tail sections with the trussing needle or paring knife and cut a design on the turtle's shell.

VARIATION

■ Cut fish shapes and use the tip of a paring knife to etch half-circle-shaped scales on the skin.

Turtle

A few clever cuts and tucks turn cucumbers into endearing crabs. Place one beside a bowl of seafood bisque or let a number of them encircle a platter of crabmeat salad. Cucumber crabs are perfect with a seafood quiche. Create a centerpiece by perching several crabs on an arrangement of shells and stones.

Select a large cucumber. Cut a lengthwise slice from one side. The slice should be about 1/2 inch at the thickest part. Place it on a cutting board, with the cut surface down.

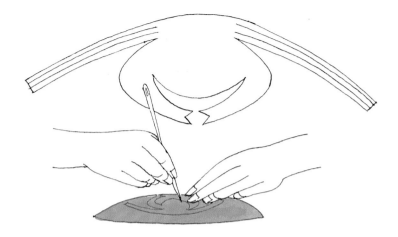

Make a paper pattern by drawing and cutting out the
silhouette of the crab and its legs, as shown. Place the
pattern on the cucumber. Draw the outline
of a crab on the cucumber with the sharp, flat tip
of a trussing needle, or a paring knife.
First draw the head, then the claws, then the sections
that will be slit to form the curved legs.

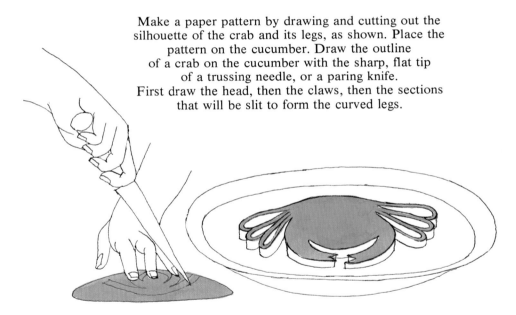

Cut along the outline, still using the tip of a trussing
needle or paring knife.

Cut slits to form the crab's legs. Tuck each of the
leg sections into a loop, forming curved legs. Soak in
ice water until ready to use.

RABBIT

Fresh, juicy orange slices can become charming rabbits with long loopy ears, eyes and a button tail. Serve with roast poultry, fruit desserts or spiced beverages. You can create 6 or 8 rabbits from a single orange. Use the rabbits in pairs or in small groupings, propped up against food or around the edge of a dish.

Choose an orange with a thick rind. Cut 3 to 4 slices, each 1/3 inch thick. Cut horizontally (not through the stem end). The number of slices you can cut from an orange depends on the size of the orange. The end sections are not used for the rabbits.

Cut each slice in half, forming half circles.

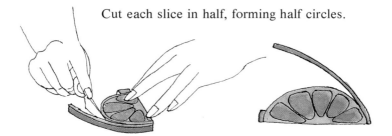

Leave a small knob of rind uncut to represent the rabbit's tail. Start 1/4 inch from the end and cut along the white membrane, separating the rind from the pulp. Cut to 3/4 inch from the edge. Leave this last section attached.

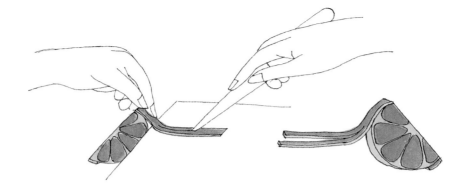

Place the strip, still attached to the orange slice,
on a cutting board. Split it in half lengthwise. Trim one
strip just 1/4 inch shorter than the other so that each ear
will show up better.

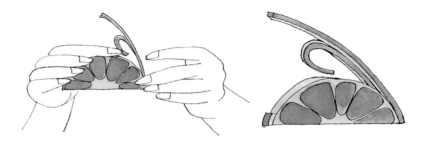

Tuck each strip in to form loops representing the rabbit
ears. Place a whole clove in the white membrane on each
side of the head to represent the rabbit's eyes.

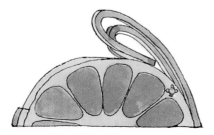

Don't let the elaborate appearance of this apple bird intimidate you. The feathers are simply three sets of concentric wedges, and the head is a slice from the base section. You will find it rewarding to make, and you can use the same technique to cut radish, pear or melon birds. These birds are at home perched on cheese trays. They can also highlight platters of roast pork with applesauce, and poultry with apple stuffing.

Cut off a slice from the side of an apple to form a flat base so that the bird will sit stable. (It will also give you a piece from which you can later cut the head.)

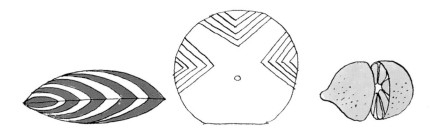

Lay the apple on its flat base. Using a knife with a thin flat blade such as a fish fillet knife or a slicing cleaver, cut a small V-shaped wedge from the top of the apple. Set it aside. Cut a slightly larger, deeper V-shaped piece from the same piece. Set it aside. Repeat cutting consecutively larger, deeper V-shaped pieces until you have 4 to 6 pieces. The number of pieces you cut depends, of course, on the thinness of the slices and the size of the apple you use.

On the right and left sides, cut another series of V-shaped pieces. Carefully set aside each piece, keeping them in the order in which they were cut.

Dip each of the pieces in lemon juice to help keep them white. Reassemble the pieces in their original order. Shingle or spread the pieces to show their outlines and form a repeated design.

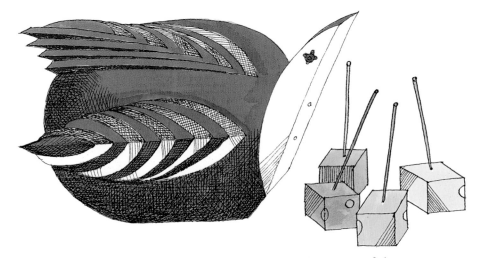

Form the head by cutting a strip from the center of the piece cut from the base. Stick 2 cloves into the cut surface to represent the eyes. Attach the head to the body either by cutting a tightly fitting channel to hold the piece, or, if the bird is for display only, by using 2 toothpicks to secure it. (One toothpick would serve as a pivot point rather than keeping the head upright.)

Bird of Paradise

SWAN

Elegant melon swans filled with fruit make beautiful individual appetizers or desserts. Two swans poised on a mirror can also form a lovely centerpiece for a dining table or a buffet table. Birds made from honeydew melon take full advantage of the fruit's delicate coloring and graceful curves.

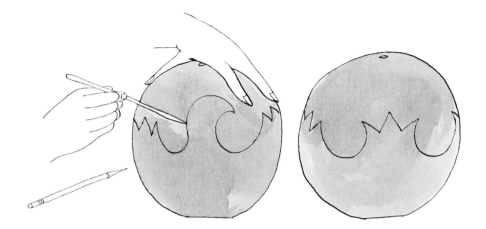

Select a melon with an unblemished rind. Trim a flat base at the stem end so that the melon sits stable on its end.

Using the sharp tip of a trussing needle or skewer as a pencil, draw the outline of a swan on the melon rind. First outline the head and neck, then outline 3 feathers on each side of the body, and finally outline a tail feather at the center back.

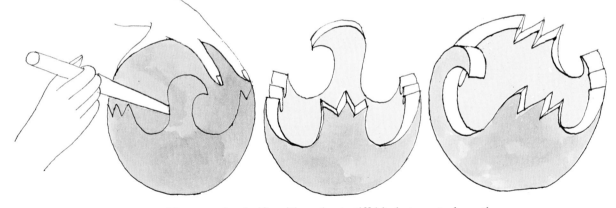

Use a paring knife with a short stiff blade to cut along the outline and remove the unwanted top section of melon. Scoop out and discard the seeds. Serve the melon as is, leaving the pulp intact, or scoop it out and fill the interior with an assortment of fruit such as honeydew, cantaloupe or watermelon balls, grapes, berries, or sections of oranges and apples.

EAGLE

Surprisingly, a watermelon eagle is simple and very fast to create. Buffet guests will find it convenient to serve themselves from it because of its large, open shape. A spread eagle helps to set a patriotic theme at festive summer picnics, particularly on Memorial Day or the Fourth of July.

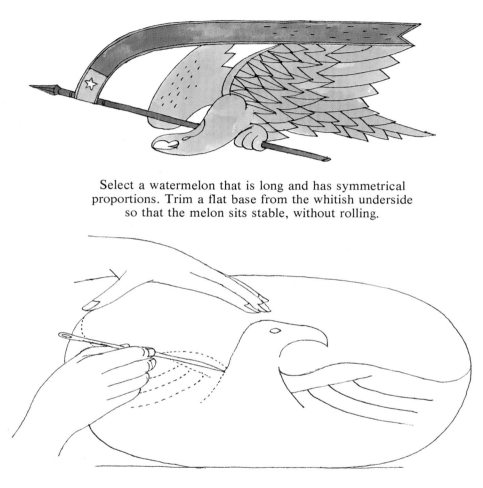

Select a watermelon that is long and has symmetrical proportions. Trim a flat base from the whitish underside so that the melon sits stable, without rolling.

With the most attractive coloring of the watermelon toward the front, draw the outline to be cut. Use the sharp tip of a trussing needle or skewer as a pencil. First draw the head and neck of the eagle, then draw a smooth, large oval opening to represent its spread wings and body.

Use the tip of a trussing needle or lemon stripper to remove a few strips of rind to represent the eagle's feathers.

Cut along the drawn outline, deep into the melon, to cut away and remove the unwanted top section. Use a grapefruit knife or spoon to scoop out the flesh from the base section.

Scrape away some rind for the face area using a vegetable peeler, and use one black watermelon seed for the eye. Secure the seed with a toothpick, cutting off any extra length.

Fill the body of the eagle with fruit.

Eagle

PEACOCK

The proud peacock is bound to be a grand pièce de resistance at any party. Its brilliant plumage is composed of fruit threaded onto wooden skewers. Plan the fruit for the feathers to make a pleasing pattern.

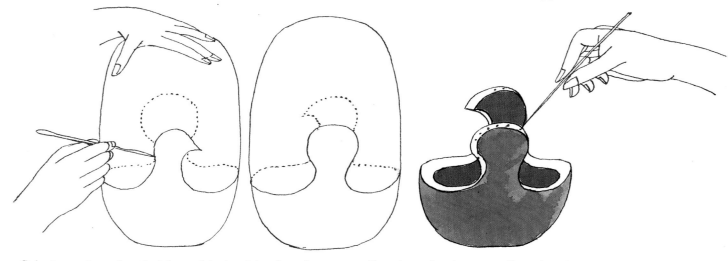

Select a watermelon that is oval but not too long in shape. The melon will be used sitting on end rather than the usual position of lying down. Trim a flat base on one end so that the melon sits upright and stable.

Place the most attractive coloring toward the front and the whitish underside toward the back. Draw the outline to be cut with a trussing needle or skewer. First draw the head and neck of the peacock, then draw the sides of the body. Finally draw the rounded center of its tail.
(Skewers will be stuck into the tail to represent the feathers.)

Cut along the drawn outline, deep into the melon, to cut away and remove the unwanted top section. Use a grapefruit knife or spoon to scoop out the watermelon pulp from the base section.

Thread a colorful variety of fruit, such as blueberries, green grapes, mandarin orange sections, red grapes, lychees or strawberries onto each of 13 10-inch skewers. Thread the fruits in the same order on each skewer. Make the peacock's crest by threading 4 blueberries onto each of 3 toothpicks.

Use a plain skewer to poke 13 evenly spaced holes in the tail section of the watermelon. Insert a prepared skewer into each hole. Insert the crest into the top of the peacock's head.

Fill the body of the peacock with fruit.

Once you have mastered the techniques of garnishing you will develop a sense of how to create your own garnishes. Whether you gradually work your way through the book, adding one garnish at a time to your repertoire, or approach it with great intensity, mastering them all at once, you will find that the total of several garnishing techniques far exceeds the sum of the parts. You will be able to mix and match ideas, adapting them to your own favorite ingredients and subjects.

Take advantage of the natural features of fruits and vegetables, just as you've seen how to use the creamy smooth honeydew skin to make a swan, the contoured shape of an eggplant to make a vase, the contrasting dark green skin and light flesh to create a cucumber turtle.

Adapt garnishes to specific themes such as card parties, graduations, birthdays, anniversaries and seasonal holidays. Let garnishes help make an occasion a memorable celebration.

It is hardly possible to go astray in creating garnishes, but here are a few guidelines to help make your creations most appealing:

■ Only materials intended to be eaten should be presented with food. Avoid combining food with decorative items such as large branches of dried herbs, fresh flowers, evergreens and leaves.

■ Inedible decorations such as ribbons, feathers, artificial flowers, plastic or paper ornaments or figurines detract from food presentations.

■ Conceal toothpicks or skewers in decorative pieces; avoid using them in garnishes intended to be eaten.

■ Keep garnishes simple. Garnishes that are contrived and over-handled are less appealing than those that seem to emerge naturally with a few effortless cuts and slices.

■ Enjoy yourself!